Life Cycles

Seed to Sunflower

Camilla de la Bédoyère

QEB

QEB Publishing

Published in the United States by
QEB Publishing, Inc.
3 Wrigley, Suite A
Irvine, CA 92618

www.qeb-publishing.com

Library of Congress Cataloging-in-Publication Data

De la Bédoyère, Camilla.
  Seed to sunflower / Camilla de la Bedoyere.
      p. cm. -- (QEB life cycles)
  Includes bibliographical references and index.
  ISBN 978-1-59566-737-3 (hardcover)
  1. Sunflowers--Life cycles--Juvenile literature. I. Title.
  QK495.C74D345 2010
  583'.99--dc22

                                    2009001119

ISBN: 978 1 59566 781 6 (paperback)

Printed and bound in China

Author Camilla de la Bédoyère
Editor Angela Royston
Designer and Picture Researcher Melissa Alaverdy

Publisher Steve Evans
Creative Director Zeta Davies
Managing Editor Amanda Askew

Words in **bold**
are explained in
the glossary on
page 22.

Contents

What is a sunflower?

A sunflower is a type of plant. Most plants have **roots**, **stems**, and leaves.

Plants grow all over the world, except in the coldest and driest places.

⇐ Most sunflowers have golden-yellow petals.

Petal

Flower

Stems grow up toward
the light. They have
leaves and flowers.

Roots hold the
plant in the soil, and
they soak up water.

Leaf

⇦ Plants need air, sunlight,
and water to grow.

Stem

Roots

The story of a sunflower

Sunflowers grow in yards and parks. Farmers also plant them in fields, so they can sell the seeds.

A seed is no bigger than your fingernail, but each seed can grow into a tall sunflower.

The story of how a seed grows into a plant is called a **life cycle**.

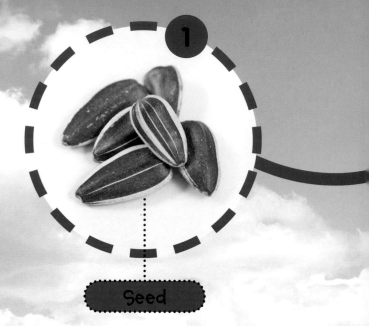

1

Seed

⇧ A sunflower has three stages in its life cycle.

2

Shoot

Flower

3

Inside a seed

A seed holds the beginnings of a new plant. It also contains food for the plant when it starts to grow.

A sunflower seed has a hard shell. It may be black, or black with cream stripes.

⇧ Seeds grow in the middle of the flower head.

⇦ If you open a sunflower seed, you can see the store of food inside.

8

This giant redwood is the largest tree in the world. It is 4,500 feet (115 meters) tall, but its seeds are tiny. Each seed is only a few millimeters long!

⇩ A redwood tree makes cones. Each cone holds many seeds.

The first shoot

When a sunflower seed is planted in soil and watered, it may begin to grow. This is called **germination**.

The seed's outer shell softens and splits open. A tiny root grows from the seed down into the soil.

⇧ The shoot grows bigger.

⇦ A shoot pushes through the soil.

⇦ The seeds are planted.

4

A few days later, a shoot begins to grow. The young plant is called a **seedling**.

⇧ The outer shell of the seed falls off.

5

⇨ Two small leaves open.

Sprouting and growing

Once the seedling has leaves, it makes its own food. The leaves use sunlight to make food from air and water.

The green leaves turn to face the sun. They collect as much sunlight as possible. Each leaf has tiny holes, which let air into the leaf.

⇨ All plants need water to make their own food and to grow.

The seedling's roots soak up water from the soil.

The seedling grows bigger every day. As it grows, new leaves appear.

⇨ A sunflower grows fastest in the first few weeks.

The flower opens

In the summertime, a green flower bud forms. The bud opens up into a big yellow sunflower.

The flower has a flat center. The center holds the male and female parts of the flower. They are needed to make more seeds.

⇧ First the green leaves open, and then the petals.

Stamen

Carpel

The male parts are called **stamens**.

The female parts are called **carpels**.

⇧ Yellow petals surround the flat center of the flower head.

Butterflies and bees

Bees, butterflies, and other **insects** are attracted to flowers. They see the bright petals, and smell their sweet **nectar**.

⇩ Nectar is full of sugar. It is food for butterflies.

Stamens are covered in a yellow powder called **pollen**. As insects sip the nectar, they are coated in pollen.

Insects carry pollen from one plant to the carpels of another plant.

⇩ Pollen sticks to the stiff hairs on a bee's legs.

Pollen

New seeds grow

Grains of pollen grow down into the carpels. They join with eggs inside the flower head. This is called **fertilization**.

When the eggs have been fertilized, they become new seeds. The rest of the flower is no longer needed, so the petals fall off.

⇨ Each sunflower head holds hundreds of seeds.

By the end of the summer, the plant looks old and tired, but it is still alive. It is growing lots of healthy seeds. The seeds swell and turn black.

⇨ The seeds are collected and used to make food for people and for pets.

Seed

Spreading the seeds

The seeds are **ripe** and full of food. They fall to the ground, or are eaten by birds.

Squirrels and mice also eat sunflower seeds. They climb up stems to reach the seeds, or collect them from the ground. They may drop the seeds, or bury them.

⇐ Birds crack open the seeds with their beak.

⤴ Squirrels hide seeds in the ground. They may come back and eat them later.

When spring comes, the seeds that are in good soil begin to germinate. They will grow into new plants, and the whole life cycle will begin again.

Glossary

Carpel
The female part of a flower. Each carpel contains an egg.

Fertilization
When a grain of pollen joins with the egg in a carpel.

Germination
When a seed begins to grow.

Insect
Small animal with six legs. Butterflies and bees are insects.

Life cycle
The story of how a living thing changes from birth to death and how it has young, or makes seeds that grow into new plants.

Nectar
A sugary liquid that flowers make to attract insects.

Pollen
Yellow dust that is made by the male parts of a flower.

Ripe
When a seed has finished growing and is ready to fall from the plant.

Root
The part of a plant that grows into the soil. It soaks up water and holds the plant in the soil.

Seedling
A young plant when it begins to grow from a seed.

Stamen
The male part of the flower. Each stamen contains pollen.

Stem
Part of the plant. Leaves and flowers grow from the stem.

Index

Notes for parents and teachers

Picture this
Look through the book and talk about the pictures. Read the captions and talk about things that have not been mentioned in the text.

Observing nature
Show children how to identify different plants that grow in the yard, park, or countryside. Look at different flowers and find the parts mentioned in this book, such as stems, leaves, flowers, and seeds.

Seed activities
Sunflowers are easy to grow in the spring and summer. Place a seed in a pot of compost, water, and leave it in a sunny place. Water it regularly. When the seedling grows, observe how it leans toward the light. As you transfer the plant to the yard, you will be able to see its roots.

Science at home
Find out how long it takes a seed to germinate and grow to full height. Keep a weekly record of the plant's growth—measure its height and count the number of leaves. Estimate how many seeds have grown in one sunflower head. Draw a sunflower life cycle with pictures of seeds, seedlings, and fully grown plants.

Family tree
Talking about a child's family helps them to link life processes to their own experience. Drawing simple family trees, looking at photo albums, and sharing family stories with grandparents are fun ways to engage young children.